CHELSEA

FOOTBALL CLUB

OFFICIAL ANNUAL 2024

Written by Richard Godden and Dominic Bliss
Designed by Adam Wilsher

g

A Grange Publication

© 2023. Published by Grange Communications Ltd., Edinburgh, under licence from Chelsea FC Merchandising Limited. www.chelseafc.com.

Printed in the EU.

Photographs © Chelsea FC; Getty Images and Alamy.

ISBN 978-1-915879-15-8

WELCOME

Welcome to The Official Annual of Chelsea Football Club!

Every true Blue is catered for in our comprehensive guide to the two-time Champions League winners, as we take you deep inside Stamford Bridge to reveal all about the greatest football team the world has ever seen.

There's so much packed into this year's Annual, with profiles of some of the huge names representing the club on the pitch and in the dugout, as well as an in-depth look at our men's, women's and Academy sides and their successes over the years.

Along with all your current favourites, we also celebrate some of the club's past glories, from Eighties heroes to the dearly missed Gianluca Vialli, along with a tribute to a pair of legendary recently departed skippers and a reminder of our incredible history at Wembley Stadium to mark the 100th birthday of the home of English football.

You can put your Blues knowledge to the test along the way too, as we've got some fiendish puzzles and quizzes to find out just how much you know about your favourite club. We hope you enjoy it and remember – keep the blue flag flying high!

Stamford and Bridget

CONTENTS

HOME SWEET HOME

THIS IS OUR

Stamford Bridge has been our home since Chelsea Football Club was founded in 1905. Okay, all of the stands have changed at some point during that time but it is still the same place, the same spirit, the same centre of everything Chelsea.

In our entire 118-year history we have only played one home game away from the Bridge, and that was a Champions League game against Porto in 2021, which was played behind closed doors in Seville, Spain, during the Covid-19 pandemic.

HOME The Pride of London

10 REASONS
WE LOVE CHELSEA!

What better way to start the Chelsea Annual 2024 than with a reminder of some of our favourite things about being a Blue...

PRIDE OF LONDON

Let's kick off with a statement sure to annoy our many rivals from the capital: Chelsea are the ONLY team from London to win the Champions League! The competition has been running in its current state since 1992, and prior to that it was the European Cup from 1955 (when we should have entered the first tournament, only to be dissuaded from doing so by the FA – although that's a story for another day). In all that time, almost 70 years, we're the only team from London to lift the trophy. What's more, we've done it twice, beating Bayern Munich in their own backyard in 2012 and then defeating Manchester City in Porto nine years later.

WE'VE WON IT ALL!

If you've ever been to a game at Stamford Bridge, you'll have almost certainly heard Blues fans chanting, "We've won it all!" And do you know what – we have! Every single competition we've entered, whether it's the Premier League, any of the domestic cups – yes, we're including the short-lived Full Members' Cup – the Club World Cup, European trophies... we've got our hands on all of them. The last few decades in particular have been a great time to be a Blue, and since 2005 we haven't gone more than two years without lifting silverware!

STAMFORD BRIDGE

As Suggs puts it in his classic Chelsea anthem, Blue Day, Stamford Bridge truly is "the only place to be every other Saturday". Okay, so it doesn't quite work in this era of wall-to-wall TV coverage with matches moving away from the traditional 3pm Saturday kick-off slot, but our west London home is so special to so many people. We've played there since the club was formed in 1905 and all but one of our home games have taken place at the Bridge – it would have been every match, had it not been for Covid – and while there have been many changes to the stadium over the years, it always feels like home.

CFCW'S DOMINANCE

Chelsea's recent success hasn't just been limited to our men's team. Emma Hayes has turned Chelsea Women into the dominant side in England over the past decade since we won our first major trophy in 2015. Visits to Wembley Stadium are almost an annual occurrence and we've won the Women's Super League and FA Cup Double three years in a row! Kingsmeadow has become like a fortress as we're backed by the best fans in the country and we've also had some massive crowds at Stamford Bridge, as women's football continues to grow year on year. All that's missing from the trophy cabinet is the Champions League, but we're getting closer...

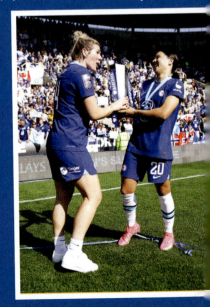

HOMEGROWN HEROES

Our Academy is among the very best in the world and as well as winning silverware regularly at youth level, there's a steady stream of top-quality footballers stepping up to the men's first team. It's been a regular feature at Chelsea since our first youth programme began in the 1950s, with the likes of Jimmy Greaves and Bobby Tambling – two of our greatest goalscorers – among the first to come through. John Terry, who will forever be known as Chelsea's 'captain, leader, legend', also emerged from the setup and in our most recent Champions League triumph, in 2021, we had no fewer than five youth graduates in the matchday squad!

WORLD-CLASS TALENT

One of the best things about being a Chelsea fan has got to be the players who put on a show at Stamford Bridge and Kingsmeadow on a weekly basis. They are the ones who are living our dream by pulling on the famous blue shirt, representing the badge that means so much to all of us; they are the ones who adorn posters on our wall, who we one day dream of emulating. We could be here all day listing some of the great players who have done this club so proud over the years. As well as the homegrown heroes we've listed on this page, there's the likes of Didier Drogba, Frank Lampard, Eden Hazard and Gianfranco Zola, each of whom gave us more magical moments to celebrate than we could have dreamed of. Chelsea Women can call upon Sam Kerr, Fran Kirby, Millie Bright and so many more who are among the very best in world football.

NEVER-SAY-DIE MENTALITY

In modern football there's a lot of talk about clubs having a philosophy or an identity, and so often that relates to playing style. What defines Chelsea, however, is a mindset that emerged back in 1970, when we upset the odds to defeat Leeds United to win the FA Cup for the first time and has become part of the fabric of the club over the past couple of decades. Time and time again, we've shown a steeliness and a will to win that has allowed us to produce some incredible comebacks, particularly in Europe, and that mentality has been behind so much of our success. Just look at our two Champions League triumphs, when few people gave us any hope of prevailing, but we somehow found a way to emerge victorious. Sometimes it can feel like a bit of a rollercoaster of emotions, but there's never a dull moment being a Blue.

LEADING THE WAY

Mauricio Pochettino is the man in the Stamford Bridge hot seat and Emma Hayes has become a club legend during her incredible tenure at the helm of Chelsea Women, and they're just the latest in a long line of incredible managers and coaches who have led the club through the years. Many of them haven't just delivered success either. We've had entertainers – who could forget Jose Mourinho's legendary "Special One" press conference, or Ruud Gullit's desire for "sexy football"? There have been innovators like Tommy Docherty and Dave Sexton in the Sixties and Seventies, and legendary ex-players such as Gianluca Vialli and Roberto Di Matteo who have led us to major trophies.

WE ALL FOLLOW THE CHELSEA!

Without you – our wonderful supporters – football would be nothing. From the chants that can be heard on every matchday, home or away, to the incredible Tifo-style banners that pay tribute to Blues legends past and present, you cheer us on through the sun and rain. Never forget that you're the heartbeat of this football club.

BLUE IS THE COLOUR

There's something special about pulling on the famous Chelsea shirt. From those who have been fortunate enough to run out onto the hallowed turf at Stamford Bridge, to those who dream and faithfully follow; kids proudly trying on that first shirt at Christmas, or playing in the park in the latest kit, pretending to be their heroes; supporters cheering from the stands, or watching from afar around the world. Football kits are an integral part of fan culture, and here at Chelsea we've been blessed with some all-time classics over the years. Something just feels so very special about those blue shirts and shorts, complete with white socks – and blue will always be the colour as far as we're concerned!

POCH!

Mauricio Pochettino became Chelsea manager at the start of this season for the latest step in his impressive football career. Let's take a look at his journey to Stamford Bridge...

PLAYING DAYS

Before he was a top manager, Pochettino was an international player as well. He got 20 caps for Argentina and played for his country at the 2002 World Cup, where he came up against an England side featuring Chelsea legend Ashley Cole.

Pochettino was a stylish centre-back, winning two Argentinian league titles with Newell's Old Boys, where his boss was former Leeds manager Marcelo Bielsa.

He moved to Europe in 1994, joining Espanyol, who are the second club in the city of Barcelona. He had two spells with Espanyol and won the Spanish Cup in each period he played for them!

Between those spells, he played in France, for Paris Saint-Germain and Bordeaux.

FIRST STEPS IN COACHING

Pochettino became a manager in January 2009, when he took charge of his former club Espanyol. He spent about four years with the club before taking his first steps in English football with a surprising move to Southampton in January 2013.

At the time, he was not well-known in England but he didn't take long to prove his worth to the Premier League audience, transforming the way the Saints played. He guided them to safety in his first few months in the job, then led them to an eighth-place finish in his first full campaign in charge.

LONDON CALLING

His remarkable achievements with Southampton were enough for Tottenham to come calling at the start of the 2014/15 season, and soon he was one of the most respected coaches in world football.

Under Pochettino, Spurs enjoyed their best spell for decades. They reached the League Cup final in his first campaign, but were beaten by Chelsea at Wembley. A year later, they challenged for the title, but were pipped by Leicester – the game that ended Tottenham's hopes of winning the league was a draw at Stamford Bridge. Chelsea again!

Pochettino led his team to second and third-place finishes in the next two seasons, and in 2018/19 he reached the Champions League final – Tottenham's first

ever – although they lost to Liverpool in Madrid.

In November of that same year, Pochettino departed after five years in North London, having taken Spurs to new heights in the Premier League era.

POCH IN PARIS

After taking a break for a year, Pochettino returned to the touchline as manager of PSG in January 2021, replacing Thomas Tuchel, who moved to Chelsea at that time. Over the next year-and-a-half, Poch won the French league title and the French Cup as well as the equivalent of the Community Shield, the Trophee des Champions.

He departed PSG in the summer of 2022 and took a year out from coaching before taking his new role at Chelsea.

BECOMING A BLUE

Pochettino arrived at Chelsea with a statement of intent and a clear aim: to return the club to winning ways.

"It's a culture of winning," he said. "In the last 10, 12, 15 years, Chelsea is the greatest team in England. I know very well the Premier League and what the culture of Chelsea means. I think our fans are excited to again be on the road of trying to win.

"We are here to try to help the club and the fans. In the end, the most important thing in football is for them to be happy and to feel proud of us and in the way we approach games.

"If we are all together, we are going to be very strong. We have an unbelievable squad and for sure are going to bring players with commitment who want to be part of it also. With the fans and everyone, we can find again the way to be successful."

ARGENTINIAN BLUES

Mauricio Pochettino might be Chelsea's first head coach from Argentina, but a few players from that corner of South America have called Stamford Bridge home over the past couple of decades. Here's all you need to know about the Argentinians who have donned the blue shirt, with an in-depth look at Enzo Fernandez over the page.

HERNAN CRESPO

Crespo is undoubtedly the most successful Argentinian to line up for Chelsea, having played a big part in helping us to win our second Premier League title in 2006.

The striker joined us three years prior to that, arriving from Inter Milan just a few years after he had been, for a brief period, the most expensive player in world football after signing for Lazio. Throughout his time in Italy, he was a prolific marksman, known for his prowess in the penalty box – and he celebrated each goal as if it was his last, which made him a huge hit with the fanbase of each of his clubs.

His Chelsea story is an intriguing one. Although he scored some spectacular goals in his maiden campaign at the Bridge, we probably didn't quite see the best of him at that time, as he struggled to adjust to life in England. After one season he returned to his adopted homeland of Italy to join AC Milan on loan for a year, when he scored twice in the Champions League final. Surprisingly he then came back to west London.

The Blues, of course, were the defending Premier League champions, and on the opening day of the season we travelled to the home of Wigan Athletic, who were embarking upon their first-ever top-flight adventure. For 89 minutes, you would have been hard-pressed to decide which side was which, so impressive was the performance by Paul Jewell's men.

Unfortunately for Wigan, they didn't have a player of Crespo's class in their ranks. Chelsea did. The end result was a breathtaking left-footed strike from distance that arrowed into the top corner. Cries of "That's why we're champions" rang out around the JJB Stadium, and the man who had scored the goal was firmly back in favour with Blues fans.

That season, Crespo played a big part in helping us retain the title, despite being rotated with Didier Drogba for the lone striker's role. No other forward in world football could match him for movement, while he could finish with his right foot, left foot or head. He lived for scoring goals, as plenty of sides found out to their cost.

Immensely popular both on and off the pitch, Crespo's desire to be in Italy led to a return to Inter Milan at the end of his second season as a Blue, initially on loan. But his contribution was never forgotten by the fans, and he still holds the club close to his heart.

"Maybe in another life I would have been at Chelsea for a long, long time," he said in an interview more than 10 years after his departure. "It's true what they say: once a Blue, always a Blue. It's like this for me. Every time I watch Chelsea, I am a fan, I want them to win lots of titles."

Position: Striker
Born: 05.07.75
CFC career: 2003-08
Apps/goals: 73/25
Fun fact: During his time as head coach of Defensa y Justicia in Argentina, Crespo managed Enzo Fernandez and together they won the Copa Sudamericana, which is South America's equivalent of the Europa League!

Position: Goalkeeper
Born: 28.09.81
CFC career: 2017–21
Apps/clean sheets: 38/14
Fun fact: Caballero had to wait a long time to make his international debut. He was first named in the Argentina squad in 2005, but it wasn't until 2018, when he was 36, that he won his first cap!

WILLY CABALLERO

During his four years at Chelsea, Caballero was rarely first choice, but his vast experience made him a great back-up keeper who pushed the No1 and provided great support for the goalkeeping unit. When he did get a chance to play, which was 38 times in all for the club, he rarely let anyone down, and he even started the 2020 FA Cup final. By the time he departed, he had lifted the FA Cup, the Europa League and the Champions League trophies, keeping 14 clean sheets for the club.

GONZALO HIGUAIN

It was the briefest of stays for Higuain at Stamford Bridge, as he spent the second half of the 2018/19 season on loan from Juventus. His pedigree could not be questioned, as he had more than 100 La Liga goals for Real Madrid and three league titles to his name, as well as setting a new single season scoring record in Serie A with Napoli. While he won the Europa League during his short stint in blue, it was far from a memorable loan spell for Higuain.

Position: Striker
Born: 10.12.87
CFC career: 2019
Apps/goals: 18/5
Fun fact: Higuain spent the last years of his playing career in the MLS with Inter Miami, where former Manchester United and England full-back Phil Neville was his head coach!

JUAN SEBASTIAN VERON

It's a shame that things didn't work out for Veron at Chelsea, as there's no doubt he was one of the most talented playmakers of the late 1990s and early 2000s during his time playing in Italy. But something about English football just didn't seem to click with the player who was nicknamed La Brujita (which translates to The Little Witch), as he also struggled at Manchester United prior to joining Chelsea in 2003. He managed only one goal in 14 appearances for the Blues and spent most of his time with the club on loan at Inter Milan.

Position: Midfielder
Born: 09.03.75
CFC career: 2003–07
Apps/goals: 14/1
Fun fact: As a young boy, Veron dreamed of playing for Sheffield United because his uncle, Pedro Verde, had been a player there between 1978 and 1981!

FRANCO DI SANTO

Perhaps it was just down to his nationality, but when Di Santo came to Chelsea in 2008 it didn't take long for people to start likening him to Crespo. He was not, however, a penalty-box predator like his compatriot – working the channels, putting himself about and grafting for the team were the things he brought to the table. Each of his 16 Blues appearances came from the bench, without a goal, but he did win the FA Cup with Wigan Athletic.

Position: Striker
Born: 07.04.89
CFC career: 2008–10
Apps/goals: 16/0
Fun fact: Di Santo has clocked up some serious air miles as a footballer. As well as appearing in England, he's also played in Chile, Germany, Spain, Brazil, Argentina, Turkey and Mexico!

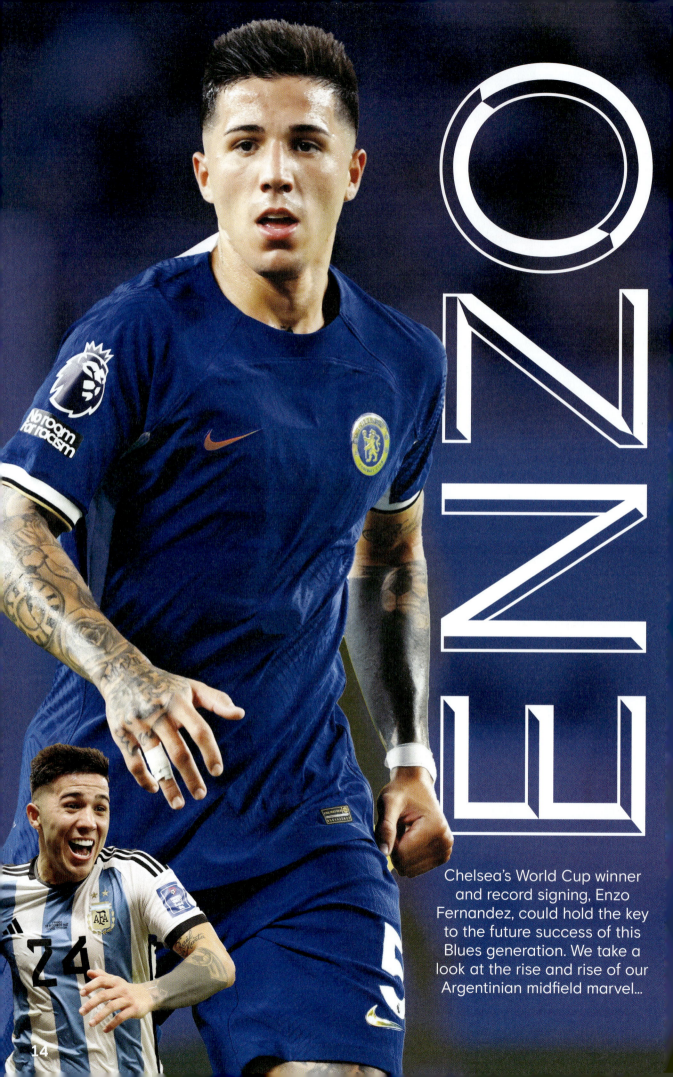

ENZO

Chelsea's World Cup winner and record signing, Enzo Fernandez, could hold the key to the future success of this Blues generation. We take a look at the rise and rise of our Argentinian midfield marvel...

14

MEANT TO BE

From the very beginning, Enzo Fernandez was destined to become a footballer. He first kicked a ball at the age of three, joined his local team Club La Recova soon after that and, by six, he was playing for River Plate, one of the giants of Argentinian football and the team his father Raul supports. He was named after a legend of the game, Enzo Francescoli – a Uruguay international and two-time South American Footballer of the Year who starred for River Plate in the 1980s and 1990s.

CHELSEA INSPIRATION

Fernandez went on loan to a club called Defensa y Justicia as a teenager, and his manager there was Hernan Crespo, the former Chelsea striker who won the league with the Blues back in 2005/06.

"He's a very special person," said Enzo. "We already know what Hernan was like as a player, he has proved it over the years, but even as a person he's a top guy, he always tries to help, always gives advice. He always has stories to tell and whenever I needed him, he was always there. He has taught me a lot on the field."

Fernandez also lifted his first trophy in that loan spell, as Defensa y Justicia won the Copa Sudamericana, the equivalent of the Europa League in South America.

When he returned to River Plate, he became a regular starter and won the Argentinian league title with his boyhood team.

"I always dreamt of achieving such a thing," he said. "I'd always attended the stadium, watched the games from the stands. Having fulfilled the dream of becoming a champion with them, that is priceless."

WORLD CHAMPION

Fernandez had gone from senior debut, to continental champion, to title winner, all before he had turned 21. Then, in the summer of 2022, he moved to Europe and signed for Portuguese club Benfica, where he settled into running the game from a deep midfield role.

His club form earned him his first appearance for the Argentina national team early last season, and by the time the World Cup rolled around in November, he was part of the squad.

He didn't start the first game, which Argentina lost to Saudi Arabia in the shock of the tournament, but he made his way into the team over the course of the group stage and quickly became one of the key players as his country were crowned world champions for the first time since 1986.

Looking wise beyond his years, Enzo was rewarded for his performances with the FIFA Best Young Player award.

"It was crazy because Argentina winning the World Cup after many years was amazing and very important for the people because they needed it a lot. We had gone through a tough period as a whole, so everybody deserved it. They were very happy, and the truth is that we were even more thrilled."

BLUE ARRIVAL

His incredible rise to the top of the game continued after the World Cup, when he was on the move again – this time to England, the Premier League... and Chelsea.

"I came to a big club, one that has always fought for titles, and that has won two Champions Leagues in a very short period of time. Now that I'm here, I've realised how big this club really is."

It was a tough first half-season at Stamford Bridge, but Enzo has faith in what we can achieve here in the future.

"One of the factors was that I liked the long-term project the club is creating. This was an important factor when making this decision, apart from the fact that it's in such a beautiful city like London. I thought it all through with my family. If it's God's will, everything will turn out fine, and I'll strive to win anything and everything."

DOUBLE, DOUBLE, DOUBLE!

Chelsea Women continue to take the domestic game by storm, and the 2022/23 season was no exception. Here's how the Blues made it three straight Women's Super League and FA Cup Doubles in a row – and a few other things we love about CFCW.

WSL CHAMPIONS

No one has been able to stop our relentless march to WSL glory over the past four seasons. There have been some valiant contenders each year, with the title race going down to the final day, but when all is said and done, there's only one team with their hands on the trophy...

We got off to a disappointing start to the 2022/23 campaign, losing on the opening day against Liverpool, but that was one of only two defeats we'd suffer in the league all year – and the other one wasn't until the spring, when we fell to Manchester City. Either side of those losses we went on epic winning runs, the type of which we see year after year from Emma Hayes' team. Man United were beaten home and away, Arsenal vanquished at Kingsmeadow on the penultimate weekend of the season. All that was left was for Guro Reiten, one of our standout attacking players all season, and Co to help put the seal on yet another title triumph on the final day at Reading. Just look at what it meant to them!

CFCW WSL TITLES
(including Spring Series):
2015, 2017, 2018, 2020, 2021, 2022, 2023

FA CUP WINNERS

Since 2015, Wembley Stadium has become like a second home for the Blues. We've played six FA Cup finals at the national stadium in that time, and victory over Manchester United last season meant we've now lifted the trophy five times. That places us third in the all-time list of FA Cup winners, and the competition has been running since 1970!

Our run to the final was tricky, as we had to see off fellow WSL sides Liverpool, Arsenal and Aston Villa to book our trip to Wembley, where we faced the Red Devils. The two clubs were also battling it out for the WSL title, but it was the Blues who took home the trophy thanks to a goal from Super Sam Kerr – she's now scored five times in three matches at Wembley!

CFCW FA CUP WINS
2015, 2018, 2021, 2022, 2023

WINNERS 2023

Vitality WOMEN'S FA CUP WINNERS 2023

Although our 2022/23 Champions League journey came to an end with a narrow defeat against eventual winners Barcelona in the semi-finals, it was thrill-a-minute stuff throughout the campaign! The most dramatic game was undoubtedly against Lyon in front of a big crowd at Stamford Bridge, when Maren Mjelde forced a penalty shoot-out by scoring from the spot with the last kick of the game and then Ann-Katrin Berger was the hero by saving two pens to book our spot in the last four!

We didn't just score an incredible 109 goals in 40 matches in 2022/23 – some of them were absolute stunners too! Erin Cuthbert, Lauren James and Sam Kerr each won WSL Goal of the Month awards, with James' solo effort against Tottenham particularly special.

Two of the unsung heroes of our 2022/23 campaign were midfield duo Sophie Ingle and Erin Cuthbert, both of whom are blessed with plenty of technical qualities but also aren't afraid to get stuck in either. As well as winning silverware with the club, Sophie was also awarded an OBE by the King!

In the first 10 years of Emma Hayes' tenure as Blues boss, we played at Stamford Bridge only twice. Last season we more than doubled that tally, as there were four matches at the club's west London home, three of which came in the Women's Champions League – including the thrilling win over Lyon!

Millie Bright is our longest-serving player, having joined the club in 2014 – and she's only just turned 30! The no-nonsense centre-half has long been established as one of the best defenders in world football and she's loved by the Blues faithful after being there for every single one of our trophy triumphs.

Although we've played a fair few games at the Bridge of late, our home is Kingsmeadow, which is in Kingston-upon-Thames. It's only a few miles away from Chelsea and it has become like a fortress – if you've not been to a game, what are you waiting for?!

EMMA HAYES

With each passing year, Chelsea Women manager Emma Hayes adds to her legacy as a Blues legend. This is why she's one of the best in the business...

BUILDING FROM THE BOTTOM

When Hayes took over as Chelsea Women manager in August 2012, a lot of hard work needed to be done. The club had played in our first FA Cup final a few months earlier, but English football was dominated by Arsenal – a club she had previously been a part of, both as a player and later as a coach when they enjoyed their best-ever season – and women's football could hardly have been further from where it is now.

"There wasn't a single member of full-time staff that worked for the women's section; let alone had an office, let alone had a desk," is how she recalled her first day in the job during an interview with The Telegraph newspaper. "The starting point was zero, and that was both terrifying and exciting all at once.

"Watching the team play, thinking, 'This is a million miles from what I've just come from [coaching in America]'. The gulf was so big. I was like, I don't know if I can go backwards. I didn't know whether I was going to do it because I thought 'this is pretty low level'."

After a year in the job, the Blues finished second from bottom in the WSL – but Hayes knew if she received the right backing, change was just around the corner...

WORLD-WISE

Although her dream of becoming a footballer was taken away at a young age by a chronic ankle injury, Hayes didn't allow herself to be consumed by the sport as she sought to do the next best thing and become a coach.

She continued her studies, gaining qualifications in European studies, Spanish and sociology, and spent time working for the local council in Camden and then her family's currency exchange business. She also travelled the world, picking up life experiences that would stand her in good stead when the coaching offers finally came in.

But it wasn't here in England that she got her big break. She took charge of the Long Island Lady Riders in the W-League at the age of 25, spending the majority of the next decade or so in America in various roles. Hayes didn't just coach – she was director of soccer operations at Chicago Red Stars and technical director at New York Flash. It was here that she learned not just how to build a team, but how to construct a club from the bottom up. Those experiences would prove crucial when the call came from Chelsea.

MENTALITY MONSTERS

When describing the mindset of her players in recent years, Hayes has been known to use the term "mentality monsters". For all the talent you need to make it in the game, you won't get very far unless you have a mindset to match it – there can be no compromise when it comes to winning.

To instil that desire in the squad, the manager has to be able to show that she too will do whatever it takes to get her hands on every piece of silverware that is up for grabs. For Hayes, that mindset was built from a young age, growing up on a council estate in Camden, when football games took place without any rules.

"I just used to play in the flats with all the boys, and we'd try to get all the girls to play as well," she says of her early experiences of the beautiful game. "It was the only thing anyone ever did. We were always playing on concrete, 20-a-side matches or whatever. You had to be tough! You had to pretend it didn't hurt."

PEOPLE PERSON

There haven't been too many players over the years who have said they didn't enjoy working for Emma. In fact, most will say she's the best manager they've ever played for, as she creates a winning team and a happy environment, pushing players to put the team at the forefront of everything. Don't just take our word for it – Niamh Charles thinks she's one of the best in the business!

"She's definitely a pioneer for the women's game," says Niamh. "On the pitch, she's an incredible coach and she's achieved so much, and we're really lucky to have her. But off the pitch, the way she speaks out and advocates for women, pushing issues forward – it's really important we have someone like that."

Chelsea Women and England legend Eniola Aluko clearly agrees. "She's a visionary and she executes that vision. I remember Emma saying to me in 2013, when I came back to Chelsea: 'Don't worry, stick with me, this club is going to win a lot of trophies.' Obviously you've seen the upwards rise since then. Emma is a huge inspiration.".

ONTO THE NEXT

There has been a steady flow of trophies arriving at Kingsmeadow since Hayes guided the club to our first major honour, which was the FA Cup in 2015. We've taken over as the dominant side in the English game, winning the WSL title six times, five FA Cups, two Continental League Cups, plus a WSL Spring Series and Community Shield. In fact, the only trophy missing in that time is the Champions League, although we've come close with a losing final in 2021 and a few semi-final appearances too.

Over the years, we've asked Emma many times to tell us which of these trophies was her favourite. And do you know what the answer is? "The next trophy. Everything we've won is special, but it's always the next trophy!"

That is why Chelsea Women have been able to dominate for so many years. Every trophy is celebrated, but the focus is always on winning more and more.

"When you get into the position of winning, you get used to it. People ask me, 'How do you keep motivation so high?' But you don't tire of winning. You just have to keep finding a different way to do it. It's normal for us because our environment is set up that way. The pressure and expectation on us is far greater. That's what comes with being champions – you have to expect that."

2,000 PREMIER LEAGUE GOALS

Chelsea became only the fourth team to reach the milestone of 2,000 Premier League goals, a figure we hit courtesy of a spectacular Mateo Kovacic strike against Leicester City in the 2022/23 season. Here are a few tricky teasers about some of the players who have helped us to that landmark. **Answers on page 63**

1 Frank Lampard has more Premier League goals for Chelsea to his name than any other player. Here he is celebrating his most famous, against Bolton Wanderers, but in which season did it win us our first-ever Premier League title?

2 We were crying out for a prolific striker throughout the Nineties, but we had to wait for Jimmy Floyd Hasselbaink to come along in the summer of 2000 for someone to bang the goals in. Which award did the Dutchman win in his first season as a Blue?

3 Juliano Belletti didn't score many, but when he did they tended to be worth the wait! Against which of our London rivals did he smash in this beauty to win our Goal of the Season award in 2008?

4 Here's Didier Drogba powering home a header on the final day of the 2009/10 season, when we beat Wigan to secure our third Premier League title. During his time as a Blue he became the first African player to reach which goal milestone in the English top flight?

5 Can you name the tricky little Belgian pictured scoring a sensational solo goal against Arsenal in 2017?

6 Only James Ward-Prowse and David Beckham have scored more Premier League goals than Gianfranco Zola via which method? The picture should give you a good idea ...

7 Belletti isn't the only Brazilian who could bang one in for the Blues – here's Oscar with an outside-of-the-boot special against QPR in 2014, which won him his second Goal of the Season award. But which of these three Brazilians never took home that prize: David Luiz, Ramires or Willian?

8 John Terry wasn't just an expert at keeping out opposition attackers – he also knew his way to goal. How many times do you think he found the back of the net in the Premier League, setting a record for most goals scored by a defender in the competition?
a) 11   b) 25   c) 41

9 This is Mick Harford, a centre-forward who scored 11 goals for Chelsea. The first of these was particularly special, in August 1992, as it was something no Blue had previously done. What was it?

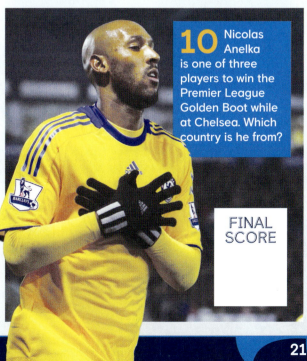

10 Nicolas Anelka is one of three players to win the Premier League Golden Boot while at Chelsea. Which country is he from?

FINAL SCORE

WHEN WE WERE YOUNG

BEN CHILWELL

I grew up in Ridgmont, a little village in Bedfordshire, and I played for the local team, called Woburn Lions from the age of six. It's a small village, a tight-knit area. I grew up with a group of friends that were really close – there were five of us who were always together and we're all still very close now.

It was all about playing really, rather than going to football. I never really supported a team growing up, although to be fair I remember asking my parents for a Chelsea shirt for my 12th birthday. That would have been the era of Frank Lampard, Ashley Cole, John Terry, Didier Drogba – they had a great team and they were winning most things, so that's probably why I asked for the shirt!

My dad, Wayne, was an important influence on me. He had a sporting background as well, although it was more rugby and cricket for him. He made me practise hard, so it was instilled in me not to do anything with half measures, so that everything I do is at 100 per cent. I often look at what he and my mum sacrificed, driving me here, there and everywhere. It was difficult, but they knew what my dreams were and thankfully helped me to pursue them.

FRAN KIRBY

Every night after school, me and a boy called Dan Martin would go down the local park and we'd be out there playing football until dinner time. Then we'd rush home, eat dinner, and go straight back to the park! I wasn't the only girl there, a few others would see me playing and then get involved.

I used to do judo and my coach said if I'd pursued it like I had football then I'd have probably gone quite far. I obviously chose football, but that was mainly because I was the only girl at the judo club I went to, so I was always fighting against boys and they got a lot bigger, whereas I stopped growing at the age of 10! I also really enjoyed being part of a team environment, rather than just being on my own.

As a young footballer, I started off really wanting to be in goal! I spent quite a bit of time playing there, but then I didn't grow at all. The coach said, "Okay, we need to put you out on pitch." So I started playing as a winger, because I was a lot smaller and quicker, and then I moved to striker.

JELENA CANKOVIC

I played football with boys when I was a kid, and actually there is a player at Fulham, Sasa Lukic, who I played against growing up, maybe when we were 11 or 12. I played against boys until I was 15. I'm from Belgrade and I was with a club called OFK Perspektiva – it was a really high level.

My biggest idol was Ronaldinho. That was the player I was really enjoying watching. As a kid, I'd watch his game, when he was doing all the tricks, and I'd go out into the back yard and try to repeat them. The main one I was practising was the flip-flap he used to do.

I also liked Thierry Henry, but he wasn't really a player I saw myself as similar too. Ronaldinho is my idol, the main player I was looking up to.

Women's football in Serbia is still not as developed as here or in a lot of countries, but I would say me playing for Chelsea really helps a lot. It gave it a lot of coverage, people are following it now, and I'm happy that my move to Chelsea can help women's football in Serbia to develop. It's in the media more, which is important.

NONI MADUEKE

As a boy, it was all football, literally. I used to play a lot in the park, or on the concrete – wherever I could kick a ball. I used to be outside doing skills until it was dark. Then it was school the next day, come back from school... and repeat!

I moved to the Netherlands when I was 16. I just wanted to break into the first team as quickly as possible. I wanted to be one of the young players in the first-team picture in Europe, and I was lucky to do that when I was 17, so people started knowing a lot about me. That was the whole point of moving there when I was that age – I wanted to make a name for myself as a young, talented player that was in the first team and doing well.

I didn't really find it that tough living abroad when I was so young, because I just wanted to play ball. I could play football every day, all the time, and I got the chance to play in the first team, so I was chuffed really.

WESLEY FOFANA

When I was growing up, we lived with my grandmother in Vitrolles – it's a little city just 20 minutes from Marseille. It's a big family – me, my cousins, my brothers and sisters, my mum – and it wasn't easy every day but we stayed strong in the family, stayed together, and enjoyed life.

In Marseille, everybody comes to play football. You don't know anyone? It's no problem! Come and play in my team! It's good, it's the real life, it's nice, and you create new friends, new personalities, because you're more open. Every person in Marseille is very open and it's nice. I lived in a quarter called Felix Pyat, and I played in the street every day after school.

My family has played a big role in my life because my family is me, and I am my family. We're very close – my family moved with me from Marseille to Saint-Etienne and followed me everywhere. That's important for me. I didn't grow up with a dad, I have two big brothers and one big sister, then after me I have two younger sisters – as well as my mum – so my role was to succeed for my family. I give my life for my family and everything I do on the pitch is for them – that's why on my social media I use the hashtag #PourEux – it means 'For Them' in French.

THIAGO SILVA

FANS' FAVOURITE

Chelsea supporters voted for Thiago Silva as their Player of the Year last season and it's no surprise. In our home game against Nottingham Forest in May 2023, there were huge crowd-surfing banners with his image on them at both ends of Stamford Bridge before kick-off. The Brazilian centre-back is one of the most popular Blues players of recent times and, at 39 years old, he is also our oldest outfield player of the Premier League era. It's an incredible story.

The fans sing, "He came from PSG to win the Champions League" and that is precisely what he did when he got his hands on the biggest trophy in European football at the end of his first season here.

"My relationship with the Chelsea supporters is hard to put into words – it was love at first sight," he said at the end of last season. "I feel really happy here."

CHELSEA TO THE CORE

Thiago joined Chelsea on a one-year contract in 2020 and has signed a new deal every year since. He continues to prove his worth on the pitch, where he is a rock at the heart of our defence, but also off the pitch, where he is a great leader and example to our younger players.

He says that is now a big part of his job at Chelsea – to be a role model and to show what it takes to reach the very top of the game and stay there, year after year.

"That's part of the reason for me extending my contract," he says, "to play alongside these young players that are hungry and have big dreams, but could use and learn from my experience as I pass on some of the knowledge that I have.

"But it's important to remember that I can't give them everything. I can't hand down all my knowledge, some things come from time and experience on the pitch."

In the end, though, it comes down to pure passion and his desire to pull on that Blue shirt again.

"I'm really proud to be at Chelsea and I just want this club to continue to be successful. It's not easy to come to a new club with not much time on your contract at the beginning and be applauded from the beginning, shown so much love."

IT'S IN THE BLOOD

Thiago is not the only one in his household to have fallen for the Blues – the whole Silva family is Chelsea mad.

His wife, Belle, is a passionate supporter, as are his two boys,

Isago and Iago, both of whom play in our Academy. Isago – the elder of the two boys – was part of the Under-14s team who won the Premier League Albert Phelan Cup last season, beating Manchester United in the final.

"The club is really important to all of us," Thiago says. "It's a mutual love. My wife, for instance, takes the underground to games and when she gets off the train, people recognise her and start to sing my name to her!

"That just shows the love that they have for us and we have for them."

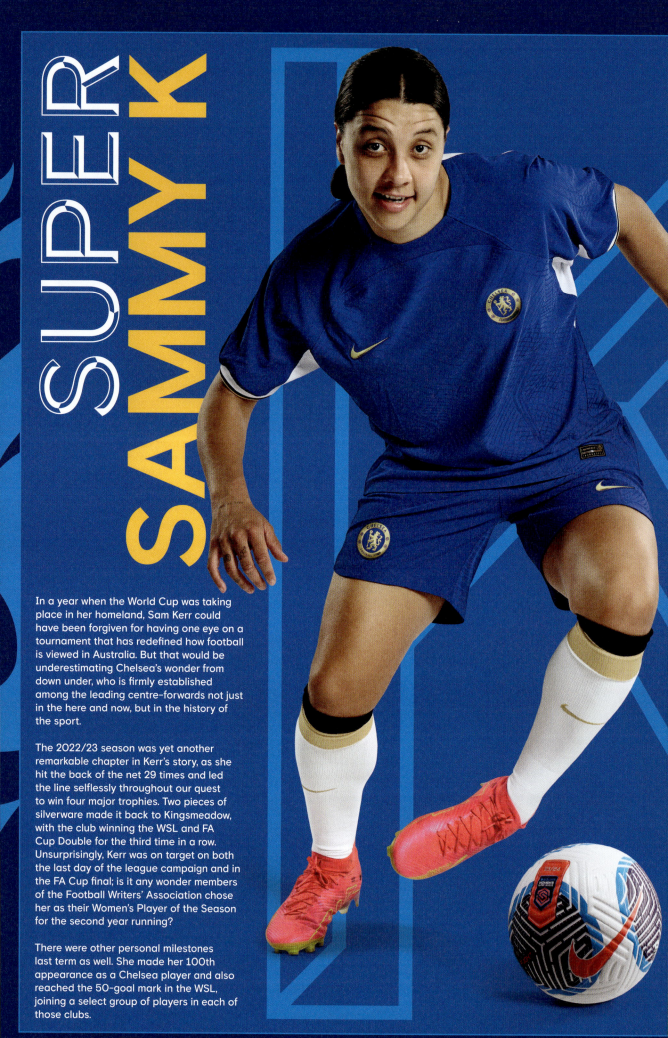

SUPER SAMMY K

In a year when the World Cup was taking place in her homeland, Sam Kerr could have been forgiven for having one eye on a tournament that has redefined how football is viewed in Australia. But that would be underestimating Chelsea's wonder from down under, who is firmly established among the leading centre-forwards not just in the here and now, but in the history of the sport.

The 2022/23 season was yet another remarkable chapter in Kerr's story, as she hit the back of the net 29 times and led the line selflessly throughout our quest to win four major trophies. Two pieces of silverware made it back to Kingsmeadow, with the club winning the WSL and FA Cup Double for the third time in a row. Unsurprisingly, Kerr was on target on both the last day of the league campaign and in the FA Cup final; is it any wonder members of the Football Writers' Association chose her as their Women's Player of the Season for the second year running?

There were other personal milestones last term as well. She made her 100th appearance as a Chelsea player and also reached the 50-goal mark in the WSL, joining a select group of players in each of those clubs.

IN HER OWN WORDS...

GREAT ENTERTAINER

"I want to be someone that is entertaining, that's fun, that scores goals, does good celebrations. I have always liked those players that have just been entertainers. I love the big-time players. I love LeBron James, Serena Williams, those players that are consistently at the top of their game. Even now I like those kind of out-there players, even if it's just their hair, their kit. But I understand being at the top level you have to do that dirty work."

DREAM TEAM

"It's an absolute dream to be part of this team. I look around and everyone is a world-class player. We have six or seven national-team captains. Every day in training there is amazing stuff being done. It's a tough environment to be part of, everyone deserves to start, so it's not easy, but that's what drives us to be the best team."

POSITIVE THINKING

"I'm really superstitious so I really don't change my schedule. I keep the same kind of routine, especially if we've been scoring and winning games. You can't think about losing ever – that's the number one sin as a footballer. Once you're thinking negative thoughts, that's the only way you're going to go so for me, I visualise scoring a goal, the celebration, seeing my family after the game – all the things that make me play football and be a footballer."

COVER STAR

"To be on the cover of a FIFA game, I kind of knew it would be a big moment – to finally have a female on the world edition – but it was much bigger than I anticipated. The reach that FIFA has... You don't realise. Everyone plays. Even non-football fans. The number of people who have come up to me and said, 'I've seen you on the cover,' who would know nothing about football otherwise, has been really cool."

HONESTY POLICY

"Emma gets the best out of me and we have a really open and honest relationship. I'm not someone that likes to beat around the bush. She just tells me how it is and I tell her how it is, and I think that we just have this mutual respect. I'm just a straight-to-the-point person. That works for her because she can just tell me exactly what she wants from me. When you have such high respect, working towards the same goals, it just works."

CHELSEA PLAYER OF THE SEASON 2022/23

SAM'S TOP THREE

She's scored plenty of goals for the Blues, but somehow Sam was able to narrow down her three favourites...

1 The chip against Arsenal in the FA Cup final at Wembley is probably going in right at the top!

2 The chest and volley against Man United on the last day of the 2021/22 season. It's a game we'd been losing in too, and it was to win the league. That was pretty special.

3 The last-minute winner against Aston Villa in the WSL in 2022. I've never celebrated a goal quite like that before, although I did tell the girls before the game that if I scored I was going to take my top off. I just didn't think it would be in the last minute, but maybe it was written in the stars!

AUSSIE ICON

Sam isn't just a Chelsea legend – she's a national icon too! At the Coronation of King Charles III she was chosen by Australian prime minister Anthony Albanese as the country's flag bearer for the first-time-in-a-generation ceremony to confirm King Charles III as British monarch, handing her a significant role among the 2,000 guests from around the world in attendance.

CHELSEA FIRSTS

Our men's team have been playing since 1905, and there have been plenty of first times over the years. Let's take a look back at some of the most significant...

FIRST MANAGER AND GOALSCORER

John Tait Robertson – remember the name. He was our first-ever manager, in 1905, but the Scotland international was still playing at the time. Robertson built the Chelsea team from scratch and then scored our first goal, against Blackpool. Not a bad way to make your mark!

FIRST SENDING OFF

In March 1910, Jimmy Windridge – one of the early superstars of the Chelsea team, who had been there since our foundation five years earlier – became the first of our players to be sent off, for an act of retaliation against Nottingham Forest's George Needham.

FIRST SUBSTITUTION

Substitutes weren't introduced to English league football until the start of the 1965/66 season, when Johnny Boyle became the first Chelsea player to come off the bench in a competitive game, replacing George Graham in the 80th minute of a 3-0 win at Fulham in August.

FIRST INTERNATIONAL PLAYER

Jack Kirwan was a rapid left-winger and one of the stars of the first-ever Chelsea team. In February 1906, he became the first Chelsea player to earn an international cap while representing the club, when he captained Ireland against England.

FIRST PREMIER LEAGUE GOAL

We played Oldham Athletic on the opening day of the first-ever Premier League season, in 1992. At 0-0 on 84 minutes, big Mick Harford thrashed one in off the bar to score our first goal in the new competition. Sadly, Oldham equalised two minutes later and it ended 1-1.

FIRST PLAYER FROM OUTSIDE BRITAIN AND IRELAND

Nils Middelboe was captain of the Denmark team that won the silver medal at the 1912 Olympics, before joining Chelsea a year later, and becoming our first player from outside Britain or Ireland. He remained at Stamford Bridge for 10 years.

FIRST CHAMPIONS LEAGUE GOAL

Our first Champions League season was 1999/2000, and if you don't include the qualifying rounds, our first goal in the competition was scored by centre-back Frank Leboeuf, whose trademark penalty earned us a 1-1 draw at Hertha Berlin in the second group-stage game.

FIRST TIME WE WORE SHIRT NUMBERS

Chelsea players didn't wear shirt numbers on their backs in a league game until August 1928, when we were one of four teams to do so. Shirt numbers were not made compulsory until 1939, and squad numbers for each player, with surnames printed above, only started in 1993.

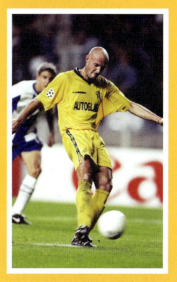

FIRST MAJOR TROPHY

The first major trophy we won was the 1955 league championship, which was called the First Division at the time, as the Premier League wasn't created until 1992. Ted Drake was the manager who led us to the title, and our captain and top scorer was the great Roy Bentley.

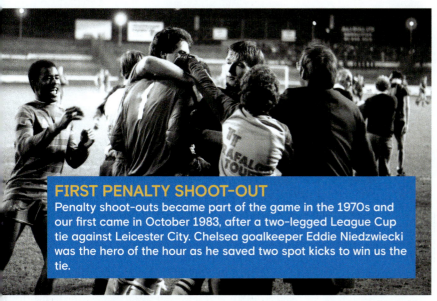

FIRST GAME IN EUROPEAN COMPETITION

Chelsea first entered European competition in 1958, and our first opponents were Danish club, BK Frem. Ted Drake's Blues won 3-1 away in the first leg, before earning a 4-0 victory at Stamford Bridge to wrap up the tie in the Fairs Cup, the first version of the Europa League.

FIRST PENALTY SHOOT-OUT

Penalty shoot-outs became part of the game in the 1970s and our first came in October 1983, after a two-legged League Cup tie against Leicester City. Chelsea goalkeeper Eddie Niedzwiecki was the hero of the hour as he saved two spot kicks to win us the tie.

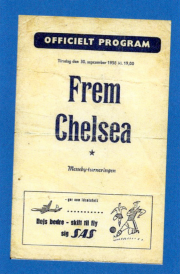

OFFICIELT PROGRAM

Tirsdag den 30. september 1958 kl. 19,00

Frem
Chelsea
★
Messeby-turneringen

- gør som Idrætsfolk

Rejs bedre - skift til fly
sig SAS

FIRST GAME UNDER FLOODLIGHTS

We made our first-ever appearance under floodlights in June 1929, at the Rua Guanabara stadium in Rio de Janeiro during a South American summer tour, but the first floodlit game at Stamford Bridge had to wait until March 1957, in a friendly against Sparta Prague.

MOISES
CAICEDO

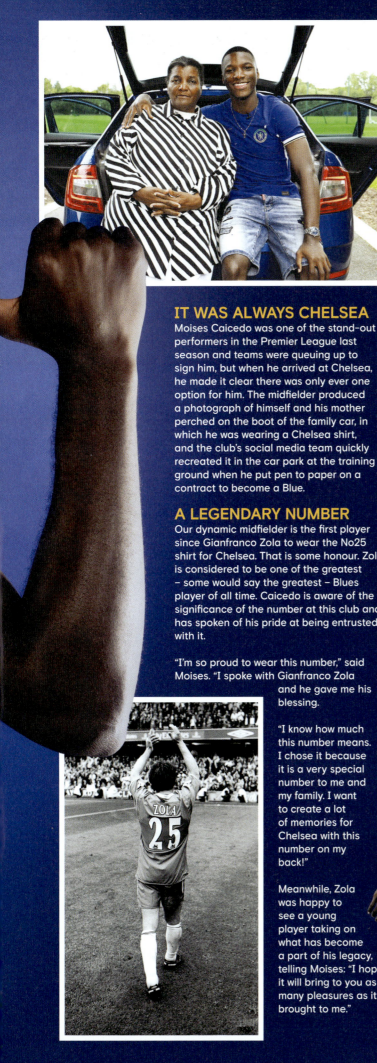

IT WAS ALWAYS CHELSEA

Moises Caicedo was one of the stand-out performers in the Premier League last season and teams were queuing up to sign him, but when he arrived at Chelsea, he made it clear there was only ever one option for him. The midfielder produced a photograph of himself and his mother perched on the boot of the family car, in which he was wearing a Chelsea shirt, and the club's social media team quickly recreated it in the car park at the training ground when he put pen to paper on a contract to become a Blue.

A LEGENDARY NUMBER

Our dynamic midfielder is the first player since Gianfranco Zola to wear the No25 shirt for Chelsea. That is some honour. Zola is considered to be one of the greatest – some would say the greatest – Blues player of all time. Caicedo is aware of the significance of the number at this club and has spoken of his pride at being entrusted with it.

"I'm so proud to wear this number," said Moises. "I spoke with Gianfranco Zola and he gave me his blessing.

"I know how much this number means. I chose it because it is a very special number to me and my family. I want to create a lot of memories for Chelsea with this number on my back!"

Meanwhile, Zola was happy to see a young player taking on what has become a part of his legacy, telling Moises: "I hope it will bring to you as many pleasures as it brought to me."

FIRST ECUADORIAN BLUE

Caicedo became the first Ecuadorian to play for Chelsea when he made his debut in August 2023. At the age of 21, he already had more than 30 caps when he joined Chelsea and was a key part of Ecuador's squad at the World Cup in Qatar, scoring in their final group-stage game against Senegal.

THE STORY SO FAR

He began his career with Ecuadorian Serie A club Independiente del Valle, before moving across the Atlantic Ocean to sign for Brighton in 2020. Following a loan spell in Belgium with Beerschot, the midfield dynamo gradually made his way into the first-team picture on the South Coast and last season he was named the club's Player of the Season by both the fans and his team-mates.

MEN'S TEAM
QUIZ

1. Which new signing bagged our equaliser against Liverpool on the opening day of this season to become the first French player to score on his debut since Kurt Zouma in 2014?

2. Which of our full-backs used to be a county-level cross country runner as a schoolboy?

3. Noni Madueke (below) was born and raised in London, but before he signed for Chelsea he had played all his senior games abroad… in which country?

4. Which Premier League club was Levi Colwill (right) on loan to last season?

5. Reece James (left) played in the same Sunday League team – Epsom Eagles – as which other Chelsea player when he was a kid?

6. Which current player joined Chelsea the month after he won the World Cup?

7. Which current Chelsea player has an MBE, awarded for services to racial equality in sport?

8. Which of our summer signings was the joint-top scorer in the German Bundesliga last season?

9. Which of the current squad is also the oldest outfield player to represent Chelsea in the Premier League era?

10. Two current Chelsea centre-backs signed from Monaco. Can you name them?

Answers on page 63

WOMEN'S TEAM QUIZ

1. Which of our players played in the 2023 Women's World Cup in her home country?
a) Sam Kerr b) Millie Bright c) Melanie Leupolz

2. When she was a kid growing up in Canada, which sport did Jessie Fleming play as well as football?
a) Curling b) Basketball c) Ice hockey

3. Millie Bright is the longest-serving player in the CFCW squad, but in which year did she debut for the club?
a) 2011 b) 2015 c) 2019

4. As a youngster, which Barcelona and Brazil legend did Jelena Cankovic idolise?
a) Rivaldo b) Dani Alves c) Ronaldinho

5. Which of these players has scored the most goals for Chelsea Women?
a) Sam Kerr b) Erin Cuthbert c) Fran Kirby

6. Who provided more assists than any other Blue in the 2022/23 WSL season?
a) Sophie Ingle b) Guro Reiten c) Lauren James

7. Which of these signings in the summer of 2023 did not join us from a French club?
a) Mia Fishel b) Catarina Macario c) Ashley Lawrence

8. Johanna Rytting Kaneryd represented which country at the 2023 Women's World Cup?
a) Sweden b) Norway c) Denmark

9. From which Midlands club did the Blues sign Hannah Hampton?
a) Birmingham City b) Aston Villa c) Nottingham Forest

10. Which member of our squad was awarded an OBE in 2023?
a) Niamh Charles b) Jess Carter c) Sophie Ingle

Answers on page 63

33

LEGENDARY

Azpi made 13 appearances for the Blues in cup finals, which is a club record! He's also one of only six players to have won the Premier League, FA Cup, League Cup, Champions League, UEFA Super Cup and FIFA Club World Cup!

HAIL CESAR!

It wouldn't be unfair on Cesar Azpilicueta to say that he arrived at Chelsea in the summer of 2012, shortly after the club's first Champions League triumph, as an unknown quantity. It's not just that a lot of the supporters didn't know much about him, apart from the fact he was a Spanish right-back who joined us from Marseille; fans couldn't even say his name, so they started to call him "Dave" (it's a joke from TV show Only Fools and Horses – ask your parents about that one)!

We quickly found out that whatever challenge was put in front of him, Azpi would face it head on. No matter the position, the formation or the head coach, the Spaniard was always an integral part of the team.

He won trophies playing at right-back, then as a left-back, before reinventing himself once more as a right-sided centre-half. On the famous night when he captained us to Champions League glory in Porto, he was selected as a right wing-back. He was the man for just about any occasion, and during his second spell as Chelsea head coach, Jose Mourinho publicly wondered if a team made up of 11 Azpilicuetas would win the Champions League!

His dependability didn't just extend to filling in the blanks on the team sheet – Azpi played every minute of every league game in our title-winning 2016/17 season, becoming only the fourth outfield player ever to do so for a victorious Premier League side. It was his second title as a Blue, to go along with all the cup competitions he won along the way.

It came as no surprise when he took on the captain's armband in 2019, going on to become only the second skipper to lift the Champions League trophy for the Blues and then the first to get his hands on the Club World Cup. That meant he had won the lot in his time at the club!

Azpilicueta passed the 500-game mark in his last season at Chelsea, more than 200 of which were as captain, and he left the club having made more appearances than any other overseas player in our history. Indeed, only five Blues have featured more for Chelsea. "It is difficult to express how I feel, it has been incredible," he said of his time at the club, before leaving for Atletico Madrid. "I feel I gave everything. I love it.

"I think it would be pretty obvious to pick the highest moment of my career, when we won the Champions League in Porto. It was my first trophy as captain. Chelsea is my home, it always will be and hopefully I can come back in a different role."

JOHN TERRY ON AZPI

"When he first came in, he made a big impression within the group, his attitude in training was one of the best I came across in football. His work ethic was incredible. He would be in the gym early, the preparation was superb. He was a real example to not only the older players within the group but the younger players in the Academy."

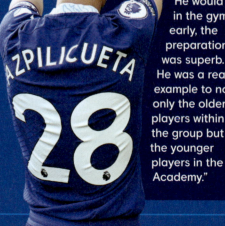

LEGACIES

It'll take some going to surpass Magda as Chelsea Women's most successful captain. At the end of the 2022/23 campaign we won our 15th major honour as a club – and Magda has lifted 10 of those trophies wearing the captain's armband!

MAG-NIFICENT!

You'll often hear football commentators wondering who writes the script for certain players – and Magda Eriksson is one of those for whom such a phrase is applicable, after her fairytale spell at Chelsea ended in a manner beyond her wildest dreams.

Not only did the popular Swede get her hands on yet another FA Cup and WSL Double, she also scored a crucial goal on her last appearance as a Blue at Kingsmeadow, helping to defeat Arsenal and move us a step closer to winning the title yet again.

Although the Champions League trophy eluded Eriksson and Chelsea, sometimes agonisingly so, during her time at the club she won every domestic honour over and over again during an incredible six-year spell.

Eriksson joined Chelsea from Linkopings in her native Sweden ahead of the 2017/18 season with a reputation as a hard-working left-back or centre-back who was a leader from a young age. She made the perfect start to life in blue, scoring on her debut against Bristol City and becoming a regular in the starting line-up in her first season, where she helped bring the WSL title back to the club.

Having been awarded the captaincy at the start of the 2019/20 season, Eriksson's first game with the armband came against Tottenham Hotspur at Stamford Bridge in front of almost 25,000 fans. Covid heavily disrupted the campaign, but we emerged with a WSL and Continental League Cup double, a feat we repeated the next season as Eriksson also became the first player to captain Chelsea Women in a Champions League final.

With a relentless desire to win, impeccable professionalism and mentality, Eriksson was a leader on the pitch and in the dressing room; the perfect team-mate and a friend to everyone. She ended up making 185 appearances, which puts her among the top 10 for the club during the WSL era and cemented herself as one of the greats to have pulled on the shirt.

"First of all, I see myself as extremely privileged to have played a part in this great club's history," she wrote in an open letter to the club's fans. "Winning was at the heart of everything we did, and that competitiveness was contagious. It's safe to say that the winning culture is now part of the Chelsea DNA.

"I'd like to thank the club, Emma [Hayes] and Paul [Green] for believing in me, and all my team-mates. Thank you for all the good times, all the competitiveness, all the support and all the love. But my biggest thank you goes to the unbelievable Chelsea fans. You will always have a special place in my heart, a place that will forever remain blue."

EMMA HAYES ON MAGDA

"There's not enough words to describe the impact Magda has had on the club. People don't really realise what this culture is unless you're in it and it's a culture where Magda, alongside me, has driven the standards. Mags has been our captain, our leader. I know the hard work that's gone on behind the scenes to get the team to where it is."

MADE IN

Chelsea love to offer our youngsters a pathway into the first tear

ARMANDO BROJA

A quick and powerfully built striker who looks to wreak havoc with his physical presence, Broja was born and raised in England but represents Albania, his parents' homeland, at international level.

After graduating from our Academy, he made his full Chelsea debut in a Premier League game at home to Everton in March 2020 and then impressed in loan spells with Vitesse Arnhem and Southampton. His return to Chelsea last season was interrupted by a bad knee injury but he'll be hoping to make an impression as he returns to action.

TREVOH CHALOBAH

The talented centre-half made a great first impression when he broke into the team at the start of the 2021/22 season, winning the UEFA Super Cup in his senior debut and then scoring on his first Premier League appearance on opening weekend.

His all-round defensive attributes make him a versatile operator and he can play at the heart of a back three or a back four, where he has also played as a right-back. He captained the team in our pre-season friendly ahead of this season, as we defeated Wrexham in the United States.

LEVI COLWILL

Two seriously impressive loan spells – with Huddersfield Town and Brighton – made this Chelsea Academy graduate one of the most talked-about centre-backs in English football when he returned home for pre-season in the summer.

His performances on the US tour backed up the hype as he impressed new manager Mauricio Pochettino during the Premier League Summer Series and was quickly signed up on a new six-year contract going into the current campaign.

CONOR GALLAGHER

Only one player made more appearances for Chelsea last season than Gallagher, who is a hard-working midfielder that runs all day for his team. He is a particularly effective runner off the ball, timing his arrivals into the penalty box to get on the end of attacking moves and catch opposition defenders off-guard.

After impressing in loan spells with Charlton, Swansea and Crystal Palace he earned his chance last season and will be looking to build on that breakthrough year in 2023/24.

COBHAM

Here's a look at the home-grown talent in our squad this season...

LUCAS BERGSTROM

An incredibly tall and imposing young goalkeeper, who has impressed in his time with the club's youth ranks, including the Under-21s squad. Last season, he took the next step in his progress by going on loan to Peterborough United, where he made his senior debut and went on to establish himself as first-choice goalkeeper for the League One side. In January 2023, he made his debut for the Finland national team in a friendly against Sweden.

He returned to Chelsea ahead of this season and was taken on the US Tour before being named in Mauricio Pochettino's first-team squad.

REECE JAMES

From a very young age, this talented all-round footballer was tipped to make it to the very top and he hasn't disappointed since being given the chance by the club he has played for from the start. James came into the side under Frank Lampard in 2019/20 after tearing up the Championship on loan at Wigan Athletic the previous year. He has been one of our star performers since, and now has the honour of being named club captain in the summer, meaning "one of our own" now wears the armband!

IAN MAATSEN

One of the stars of the pre-season tour to the USA, Maatsen lit up the left-side of Burnley's promotion-winning team during a loan spell up north last season. Now he has come back to Stamford Bridge, where he made his senior debut in a 7-1 League Cup win over Grimsby Town back in 2019. He then stood out during loan spells with Charlton and Coventry, before stepping up to another level with the Championship-winning Clarets last season.

PLAYERS TAKE THE LEAD

The Chelsea Academy has always been known for thinking outside the box and leading the way in new ideas.

At the end of last season, Under-21s head coach Mark Robinson arranged a two-legged match against Monaco to give our young players the experience of playing in a big European tie. He even told them to consider it a rematch of the famous Champions League semi-final between Chelsea and Monaco in 2004, when we were pipped to the post by our opponents.

But there was an added twist to the build-up for the second leg at Chelsea, when he asked the players to plan the preparation for the game themselves, without the coaches!

"It went really well," Robinson said afterwards. "The players were involved in taking training for the two days leading up to the game, they shared tactical knowledge together, prepared the kit and got everything ready for the game. They then took charge of the game without any coaching input, although we were there for support if needed, and it was a really good experience for everyone."

In the end, we lost the tie on a penalty shoot-out but it was all about the lessons learned by the players, who now realise what goes into the preparation for every game. It's fair to say they're very grateful for the work the staff do for them now they've had a go themselves!

COACHING STAFF

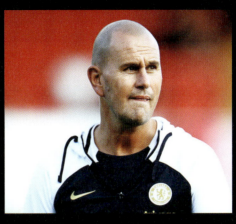

MARK ROBINSON
UNDER-21S HEAD COACH

Mark Robinson – known as 'Robbo' to his fellow coaches – took over as head coach of our Under-21s squad at the start of the 2022/23 season. He was previously in charge of the first team at AFC Wimbledon, where he spent 18 years in total, having also coached in many roles in their academy.

HASSAN SULAIMAN
UNDER-18S HEAD COACH

Hassan Sulaiman stepped up to take charge of the Under-18s in March 2023. Before that, he was head coach of our Under-16s side. He has coached in the Chelsea Academy since 2008 and knows many of the players he is now coaching from his experience working with other age groups.

GIANLUCA
VIALLI
1964-2023

A CHELSEA LEGEND

Chelsea lost one of the greatest figures in the club's history in January 2023. Luca Vialli was a fans' favourite during a magical time at Stamford Bridge, enjoying great success as both player and manager in the late 1990s and early 2000s...

ARRIVAL OF AN ICON

Gianluca Vialli signed for Chelsea in the summer of 1996, just after the Italian superstar had won the Champions League as captain of Juventus. At that time, we hadn't won a trophy for 25 years. It was an incredible signing for us – the kind we could only have dreamed of a few years earlier.

Luckily, we had a new manager who was also a former World Footballer of the Year – Ruud Gullit. Every player in the world wanted to work with Gullit, and Vialli was no different. This was a transfer that showed Chelsea were serious about competing for titles again.

CHEER UP LUCA, WE LOVE YOU!

Vialli was a striker and a natural goalscorer. Not long after joining Chelsea, he had scored crucial goals away at both Arsenal and Manchester United to announce himself on the scene.

But there were tough times for him too, as fellow strikers Mark Hughes and Gianfranco Zola formed a great partnership up front, forcing Gullit to leave Vialli on the bench often. He continued to work hard and score goals when given the chance, but it was a difficult time for him. His fans and his team-mates helped him through it – singing his name and showing him how important he was. Our captain at the time, Dennis Wise, celebrated one goal by revealing a vest with a message written on it: "Cheer Up Luca, We Love You!"

Vialli and his team-mates ended that year as FA Cup winners at Wembley – the first of six trophies he lifted with Chelsea.

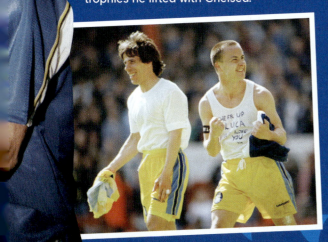

INTO THE DUGOUT

Halfway through Vialli's second season with Chelsea, Gullit was sacked and the board asked Luca to become player-manager.

He was an instant success in the new role, guiding us to a League Cup triumph at Wembley – beating Middlesbrough, who were also our victims in the previous year's FA Cup final – and then tasting European success as we ended the 1997/98 season with the Cup Winners' Cup in our hands.

SERIAL WINNER

Vialli continued to push for progress at Chelsea. At the beginning of the 1998/99 season, we beat Real Madrid to win the UEFA Super Cup for the first time in our history, and then went on a Premier League title challenge. In the end, we finished third, but we qualified for the Champions League and suddenly Chelsea were one of the top sides in Europe.

The fans loved the personality that Vialli brought to the club and 1999/00 was a memorable season as we reached the quarter-final of the Champions League, finally losing to Barcelona after extra time. We forgot about that disappointment quickly and went on to win the last FA Cup final at the original Wembley. The next season's Community Shield gave us one last glory day at the famous home of football, before it was knocked down and rebuilt into the stadium we know today.

BLUES HERO

Sadly, the next season didn't start how we would have wanted and Vialli's time at Chelsea came to an end five games into the 2000/01 campaign. The supporters loved him and were heartbroken when he was sacked. They continued to chant his name at home games for weeks after he left the club and, when he passed away in January 2023, those chants returned to Stamford Bridge. He never forgot the love of the Blues fans, and we will never forget the great Gianluca Vialli.

"I always had a fantastic relationship with the fans," he said. "They appreciated the fact that I signed for Chelsea in the first place and then, when I went through a difficult time, they were so supportive. "They loved what we did while I was manager and one of my fondest memories is that relationship I had with the fans here."

100 YEARS OF WEMBLEY

Wembley Stadium celebrated its 100th birthday in 2023, and Chelsea have enjoyed more than our fair share of memorable moments at the famous old venue in north-west London. Let's take a look at some of them...

THE ORIGINAL WEMBLEY

1944

Our first trip to the national stadium came about during the Second World War, when we reached the Football League Cup South final against Charlton Athletic. Here's an incredible colourised photo of our captain John Harris shaking hands with his opposite number before the game, which we sadly lost 3-1, although we were back the next year to beat Millwall 2-0 in the final of the same competition.

1970

One of our most famous trips to the old Wembley, with its famous Twin Towers, was for the 1970 FA Cup final against rivals Leeds United. The Blues fans were in fine voice as we drew 2-2, before winning the replay at Old Trafford a few days later to lift the game's oldest trophy for the first time in our history.

1997

It was another 27 years before we won the FA Cup again, although there were Wembley moments in between. Roberto Di Matteo scored in the first 43 seconds of the 1997 FA Cup final against Middlesbrough, and Eddie Newton added a second to make sure we took the cup back to the Bridge.

THE OLD AND THE NEW

At the start of the new Millennium, Chelsea made a bit of history that can never be broken, when we won the last-ever FA Cup final at the original Wembley in 2000, then won the first-ever final at the newly rebuilt stadium seven years later!

Dennis Wise took his baby son Henry up the steps to the Royal Box when he lifted the Cup in 2000, making it a moment nobody could forget. When we returned in 2007, it was to a new-look Wembley with an iconic arch over the top of the pitch. Didier Drogba scored the winning goal in that year's final against Manchester United.

WINNING HABIT

Chelsea Women played and won the first Women's FA Cup final at Wembley in 2015, when Ji So-Yun's goal saw off the challenge of Notts County, giving Emma Hayes the first of five FA Cup successes at the stadium.

The most recent triumph came last season, when Sam Kerr got the winner against Manchester United before joining Erin Cuthbert, Millie Bright and Guro Reiten for a celebratory selfie on top of the club crest on the dressing room floor!

CHELSEA AT WEMBLEY

Chelsea's men's team have played at Wembley on 46 occasions. Check out the complete record below.

Date	Opponent	Match	Score
15 Apr 1944	Charlton Athletic	Football League Cup (South) final	1-3
07 Apr 1945	Millwall	Football League Cup (South) final	2-0
20 May 1967	Tottenham Hotspur	FA Cup final	1-2
11 Apr 1970	Leeds United	FA Cup final	2-2
04 Mar 1972	Stoke City	League Cup final	1-2
23 Mar 1986	Manchester City	Full Members' Cup final	5-4
25 Mar 1990	Middlesbrough	Full Members' Cup final	1-0
09 Apr 1994	Luton Town	FA Cup semi-final	2-0
14 May 1994	Manchester United	FA Cup final	0-4
17 May 1997	Middlesbrough	FA Cup final	2-0
03 Aug 1997	Manchester United	FA Charity Shield	1-1
29 Mar 1998	Middlesbrough	League Cup final	2-0
09 Apr 2000	Newcastle United	FA Cup semi-final	2-1
20 May 2000	Aston Villa	FA Cup final	1-0
13 Aug 2000	Manchester United	FA Charity Shield	2-0
19 May 2007	Manchester United	FA Cup final	1-0
05 Aug 2007	Manchester United	FA Community Shield	1-1
24 Feb 2008	Tottenham Hotspur	League Cup final	1-2
18 Apr 2009	Arsenal	FA Cup semi-final	2-1
30 May 2009	Everton	FA Cup final	2-1
09 Aug 2009	Manchester United	FA Community Shield	2-2
10 Apr 2010	Aston Villa	FA Cup semi-final	3-0
15 May 2010	Portsmouth	FA Cup final	1-0
08 Aug 2010	Manchester United	FA Community Shield	1-3
15 Apr 2012	Tottenham Hotspur	FA Cup semi-final	5-1
05 May 2012	Liverpool	FA Cup final	2-1
14 Apr 2013	Manchester City	FA Cup semi-final	1-2
01 Mar 2015	Tottenham Hotspur	League Cup final	2-0
02 Aug 2015	Arsenal	FA Community Shield	0-1
22 Apr 2017	Tottenham Hotspur	FA Cup semi-final	4-2
27 May 2017	Arsenal	FA Cup final	1-2
06 Aug 2017	Arsenal	FA Community Shield	1-1
20 Aug 2017	Tottenham Hotspur	Premier League	2-1
22 Apr 2018	Southampton	FA Cup semi-final	2-0
19 May 2018	Manchester United	FA Cup final	1-0
05 Aug 2018	Manchester City	FA Community Shield	0-2
24 Nov 2018	Tottenham Hotspur	Premier League	1-3
08 Jan 2019	Tottenham Hotspur	League Cup semi-final first leg	0-1
24 Feb 2019	Manchester City	League Cup final	0-0
19 Jul 2020	Manchester United	FA Cup semi-final	3-1
01 Aug 2020	Arsenal	FA Cup final	1-2
17 Apr 2021	Manchester City	FA Cup semi-final	1-0
15 May 2021	Leicester City	FA Cup final	0-1
27 Feb 2022	Liverpool	League Cup final	0-0
17 Apr 2022	Crystal Palace	FA Cup semi-final	2-0
14 May 2022	Liverpool	FA Cup final	0-0

Chelsea Women played at Wembley for the first time in 2015, and we have been regulars there since. Last season's FA Cup triumph under the arch took it to seven appearances.

Date	Opponent	Match	Score
01 Aug 2015	Notts County	FA Cup final	1-0
14 May 2016	Arsenal	FA Cup final	0-1
05 May 2018	Arsenal	FA Cup final	3-1
29 Aug 2020	Manchester City	FA Community Shield	2-0
05 Dec 2021	Arsenal	FA Cup final	3-0
15 May 2022	Manchester City	FA Cup final	3-2
14 May 2023	Manchester United	FA Cup final	1-0

FAMILY PRIDE

Lauren and Reece James are history-makers for both club and country – and the best is still to come. Find out all about Chelsea's brother and sister superstars, as well as a quick history lesson about some of the other Blues siblings over the years.

Lauren's story so far

After starting out in Chelsea's youth system, Lauren moved on to Arsenal and then Manchester United, where she made history after scoring the Red Devils' first-ever WSL goal. But it was a return to the Blues, in the summer of 2021, that helped elevate her to the top of the women's game and in the 2022/23 season she became a star for club and country.

"I've always loved Chelsea," she says. "Even when I left and went on a different adventure for a few years, I always knew that I could come back here. It definitely feels like home and it's always been the place I've wanted to be at. It's hard to put into words how much a club can mean to someone, but it's a club that I love."

The 2022/23 campaign was her breakthrough at the top level, as she helped us to win the WSL and FA Cup with some dazzling displays on the wing. Her solo goal against Tottenham was one of the best of the season and along the way she made the step up to the international stage. She was chosen in England's World Cup squad and was one of the stars of the group stage, scoring three times and providing as many assists. Although she was sent off in the last 16 against Nigeria, James had lit up the biggest tournament in world football.

Reece's story so far

While many Blues fans will recall Reece starring in Youth Cup triumphs in his late teens, his Chelsea career began long before that. He was training with the club from the age of six! A loan move to Wigan Athletic in the 2018/19 season showed he was ready to make the step up to our first team and he's been a key player on the right-hand side, whether at full-back or wing-back, ever since.

"This is the club I want to play for, and I have worked very hard to get to this point," he said after breaking through. "I always felt that my ability was good enough and I'm just thankful that the gaffer has given me the chance to play."

DID YOU KNOW?

When Lauren made her Lionesses debut in September 2022, the James family wrote their own chapter in the history of English football, as they became the first siblings of different genders to play in senior matches for England!

He scored on his Chelsea debut against Grimsby Town in September 2019 and after a stunning debut season, the following campaign he joined the pantheon of greats at Stamford Bridge by playing a pivotal role in our Champions League triumph. Ahead of the 2022/23 campaign, Reece was chosen as only the seventh permanent Chelsea captain in the Premier League era.

Reece has also been a regular on the international stage and he was part of the England squad that reached the final of the European Championship in 2021, although he missed the World Cup a year later through injury.

Reece on Lauren

"I started playing because my older brother Josh played, and Lauren played because I played. We all used to play every day together at the park and over time we all gradually got better. When we were growing up it was both of our dreams to one day play for Chelsea and England. That achievement is now ticked off, and it's a great achievement, something we've always wanted to do and now we're finally here. I know how hard she's worked, and it hasn't been easy for either of us. It has taken her a lot of hard work to get to where she is."

Lauren on Reece

"Both of us are supportive of each other, where I will go to his games, and he will go to my games when he can. We kind of leave each other to it though. Anything to do with football, we both know what we need to do so we just leave the other one to it. But outside of football, we have a great relationship and we are really close. I think with our age gap that helps, with it only being two years. He is a funny guy!"

Lauren and Reece James might be the only brother and sister to represent Chelsea, but they're not the only Blue siblings. Here are a few more from years gone by...

Allan and Ron Harris (combined CFC apps: 897)

Allan was the older of the two, but it's Ron (whose nickname was Chopper) who takes credit for 795 of their combined apps, which remains a club record to this day!

John and Peter Sillett (390)

The defensive duo played for Chelsea in the 1950s, and Peter scored a crucial penalty to help us win the title in 1955!

Eden, Kylian and Thorgan Hazard (352)

While Kylian and Thorgan only played youth football here, Eden became an all-time Blues legend in his seven years at the Bridge. He won our Player of the Year award four times!

Graham, Ray and Stephen Wilkins (347)

Butch, as Ray was known, remains our youngest-ever club captain, while Graham was a steady defender. Their brother Stephen didn't make it into the first team, but he played in non-league.

Nathaniel and Trevoh Chalobah (93)

Trev introduced himself to Blues fans with a stunner on his home debut against Crystal Palace and Nathaniel was part of the Premier League-winning squad in 2017.

WHERE ARE STAMFORD AND BRIDGET?

Our mascots Stamford the Lion and Bridget the Lioness love celebrating with their friends and fellow fans. Can you spot them in the crowd at the opening match of the 2023/24 season at Stamford Bridge?

NEW IN BLUE

Among the new signings made by Chelsea Women last summer were Ashley Lawrence, Catarino Macario, Hannah Hampton and Mia Fishel. Find out about their game in their own words, as well as getting the low down on the quartet from Emma Hayes

ASHLEY LAWRENCE

Modern full-back

"I would define myself as a modern day full-back, adding a lot of dynamic on the field. Defensively, I'm relentless! I love one-v-one battles and I have a lot of experience with the Canadian national team and playing with another top club in Europe, defending against top strikers and wingers. On the flip side, going forward putting in quality crosses, being box-to-box and dominating out wide."

Carefree

"Growing up, playing football, I just remember the feeling that I had every time I played. It was just pure joy. Every time I stepped on the field, I was the happiest young girl – and I never want to lose that feeling of not having a care in the world and just loving the game and enjoying myself out there."

EMMA SAYS:
"Ashley has established herself as one of the best full-backs in the women's game for both club and country. Her ability to get forward, her progressive play into the final third is a standout strength and she can play on both the left and right side."

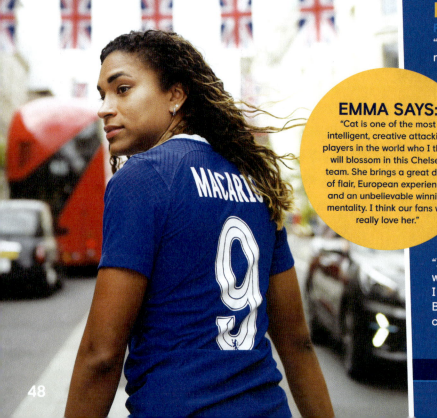

CATARINA MACARIO

Forward thinking

"I can play either as a No10 or a more traditional No9 and I think I can offer plenty to the team, which is already full of top players. I see myself making lots of link-ups with the other attackers here. I'm very fortunate that I've had some experience of playing for Lyon, a team that had many world-class players, and we won the Champions League."

EMMA SAYS:
"Cat is one of the most intelligent, creative attacking players in the world who I think will blossom in this Chelsea team. She brings a great deal of flair, European experience, and an unbelievable winning mentality. I think our fans will really love her."

Samba culture

"I got into football because I was watching my older brother play and I wanted to follow in his footsteps. Being born in Brazil, it's part of our culture, everybody plays."

HANNAH HAMPTON

Front to back

"I lived in Spain when I was younger and it was very normal for boys and girls to play together in the playground. I started out as a striker, loved it – then one game the keeper got injured so I volunteered to go in goal. After one game I got scouted by England! So I stuck with it."

Dream come true

"I just want to keep improving and help the team out in any way possible, and obviously winning trophies along the way. I started out at Birmingham, made my debut at 16, but when anyone asked where I wanted to end up it was always Chelsea. It's a dream come true."

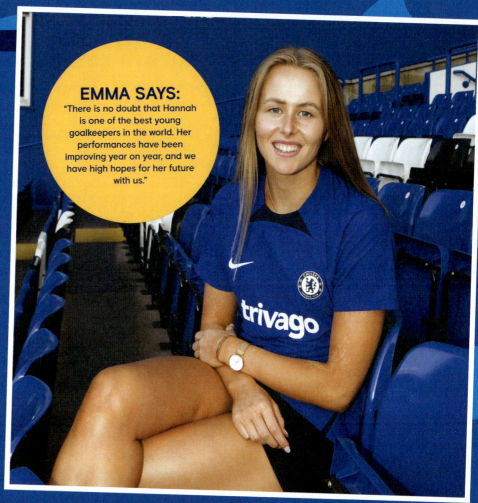

EMMA SAYS:
"There is no doubt that Hannah is one of the best young goalkeepers in the world. Her performances have been improving year on year, and we have high hopes for her future with us."

EMMA SAYS:
"She's an exceptional finisher whose box presence and movement make her elite. She can also create something from nothing and her prime years are to come. We really think she's at a great age to take this next step in her career."

MIA FISHEL

Sky's the limit

"I want to become the best soccer player here. I want to win titles, I want to win championships, I want to play in the Champions League and dominate. My ambition, just like this club, is to be the best."

True Blue

"I have been a Chelsea supporter since I was about seven years old. My brother and my dad would put on the Premier League and I would be like, 'Chelsea is my team,' and Eden Hazard was my favourite player growing up. Growing up, this was the team that made me who I want to be. The competitiveness, the wanting to win – I want to be part of this history."

49

"We're the boys in Blue, Division Two — and we won't be here for long!"

We've seen Chelsea lift every major trophy over the past couple of decades, but it hasn't always been like this at Stamford Bridge. That's why, for many of the supporters who were there to witness it, the 1983/84 season is up there with the very best years to be a Blue, as we emerged from the darkest period in our history...

Pre-1983

We were champions of England in 1955, FA Cup winners in 1970 and then the Cup Winners' Cup was lifted a year later. But just a few years after our first-ever European triumph, the Blues were down in the second tier of English football and potentially on the verge of going out of business had we not avoided another relegation by the skin of our teeth in 1983. It was tough to see how the club would emerge from the darkness...

What changed?

John Neal was our manager, and many would have said at the time he had taken us backwards. Yet the club offered him significant backing in the summer of 1983, with his previous jobs at Wrexham and

Middlesbrough showing that he knew what he was doing. After four years languishing in the second tier, the gaffer ripped it up and started again. Out went eight players, many of them established pros, and in came a whole host of unknown quantities. Kerry Dixon, Pat Nevin, Joe McLaughlin, Eddie Niedzwiecki, Nigel Spackman, each of them to become a club legend, joined that summer; John Hollins, already a Bridge hero from the Seventies, returned for one last hurrah.

Off to a flier

When the Blues dispatched of promotion favourites Derby County 5-0 on the opening day of the 1983/84 season, optimism flooded back to Stamford Bridge. By mid-November, a 4-0 thrashing of another

highly fancied club, Newcastle United, forced the rest of the division to stand up and take notice of Neal's side – but there were still signs it was not the finished article.

The spark

In early-December, a dressing room dust-up between Dixon and the lively David Speedie, who many would say could start an argument in an empty room, proved to be the catalyst for one of the club's most prolific strike partnerships of all time, with the assists coming from the jinky Nevin on the right wing.

Thinking outside the box

Although we entered the new year second in the standings and in good shape for promotion, Neal still hadn't quite completed his Chelsea puzzle. He came up with an ingenious plan, moving centre-forward Colin Lee, who was barely featuring, to right-back and that left us with one of the tallest, and least compromising, back fours in the league.

The other change to the side came in the form of Mickey Thomas, the loveable rogue who travelled from club to club, spending enough time with each to become the hero but never staying long enough to turn into a villain. It's unlikely he ever attained cult-hero status at any of his 12 clubs quite as quickly as he did at Chelsea, though, as he marked his home debut against Sheffield Wednesday with a brace in a 3-2 win which saw us overthrow the Yorkshire side atop the Division Two standings.

Unstoppable

From 2 January against Middlesbrough, the game which preceded Thomas' arrival, right the way through to the end of the season, we didn't lose another league game, and everyone was contributing. The defence, with the imperious Niedzwiecki behind them, was watertight. Spackman and club stalwart John Bumstead

provided stability and, in the latter's case, a steady supply of goals from midfield. On the flanks, Thomas offered perpetual motion and no small amount of quality. Nevin was the Player of the Year, setting up countless goals and banging in plenty of his own, including seven in the final 10 games; not forgetting the lightning pace and goal threat of Paul Canoville when he was called upon. Then, up front, Dixon and Speedie had developed into perhaps the best partnership in the country. It was just the perfect mix.

The clincher

Promotion looked to be an inevitability, and it was secured with three games to spare on an incredible afternoon against our old rivals Leeds United, who were thumped 5-0. The fans were desperate to join in the fun, invading the pitch numerous times to celebrate, and some of the pictures after the game are among the most iconic seen at Stamford Bridge.

A trip to Blundell Park to take on Grimsby Town was a fitting end to the season for the club. With all due respect to the Mariners' Cleethorpes-home, it symbolised five dark years in the Blues' history, all of which were spent away from English football's top table.

Those years, however, were now consigned to the past; this final game was an opportunity to return to the top flight with a first piece of silverware for 13 years and allow supporters to say cheerio to Division Two in style. Chelsea were champions of the second tier and it was the perfect end to a perfect season. To the merry band of Blues supporters who followed the club to all corners of the country, little can surpass the fun and games of the 1983/84 season.

WORLD CUP
BLUES

With no fewer than 19 players in action at the Women's World Cup in Australia, Chelsea Women had a huge role to play in the festival of football Down Under. Here's how the Blues lit up the biggest stage in the international game.

LIONESSES JUST MISS OUT

After winning the European Championship on home soil, England had high hopes of adding the World Cup trophy to their legacy. Five Chelsea players were in Sarina Wiegman's squad, led by Millie Bright, who skippered the side in the absence of Leah Williamson and became just the second player to lead out an England team in a World Cup final after Bobby Moore. Alas, it ended in heartbreaking defeat at the hands of a savvy Spain side, who were crowned world champions for the first time after a 1–0 victory in front of 75,000 supporters in Sydney.

Bright was a mainstay of the side throughout the tournament, as was her defensive colleague Jess Carter, both of whom were integral to the Lionesses' run to the final as they cruised through the group stage and saw off Nigeria, Colombia and hosts Australia in the knockout rounds.

Although Lauren James' tournament was temporarily halted by a red card in the last 16, she was England's standout player in their group matches, scoring three times and adding three assists. Only five players netted more goals than her at the tournament.

Niamh Charles and Hannah Hampton were also part of the squad, with the former featuring in the group win over China.

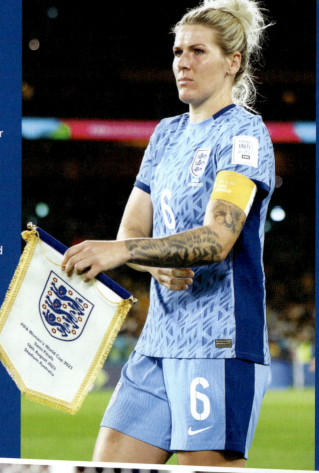

BRONZE FOR SWEDEN – AGAIN

After finishing third in France four years ago, Sweden repeated the trick once more by claiming another bronze medal with a win over Australia in the third-place play-off. One of their star players was Zecira Musovic, whose performance in the last-16 win over USA was one for the ages, as she made an incredible 11 saves to help end their eight-year hold on the trophy. It was also a single-game World Cup record for a goalkeeper who kept a clean sheet.

The Scandinavian country also had Johanna Rytting Kaneryd in their ranks, with her pace down the wing proving crucial to their run to the last four.

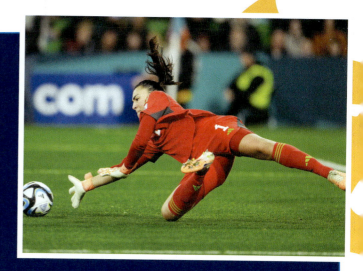

KERR LATE TO THE PARTY

An injury on the eve of the World Cup meant that Sam Kerr had to bide her time to make an impact at a tournament that she was one of the faces of, with her status as arguably Australia's greatest-ever player.

She didn't appear until the knockout stages, which the Aussies struggled into, but she showed her class in the semi-final against England with a world-class strike that was undoubtedly one of the goals of the tournament. It wasn't enough to get her team into their first final, but it was a moment she'll never forget.

IT'S A KNOCKOUT

Of our 19 players at the tournament, representing nine different nations, 13 of them made it through the group stage and into the last 16. Aniek Nouwen, Maika Hamano and Eve Perisset were all quarter-finalists with the Netherlands, Japan and France, while Guro Reiten and Maren Mjelde bowed out with Norway in the first knockout round, despite a goal from the impressive Reiten in their defeat.

SHOCK EXITS

It was a tournament to forget for our German trio of Melanie Leupolz, Ann-Katrin Berger and Sjoeke Nusken, along with the three Canadian Blues Jessie Fleming, Kadeisha Buchanan and Ashley Lawrence. Germany were Euros finalists in 2022, while Canada won Olympic gold a year earlier, but both sides bowed out of the World Cup in the group stage.

PAST.
PRESENT.
PROUD.

FOLLOW IN YOUR FAVOURITE
LEGEND'S FOOTSTEPS ON THE
STAMFORD BRIDGE STADIUM TOUR

THE PRIDE OF LONDON

SEARCH **CFC TOURS**
TO BOOK YOUR VISIT

BLUES AT THE EUROS

The men's European Championship is taking place in Germany in 2024, with plenty of Chelsea players likely to be in action, but how have Blues previously got on in the tournament?

1996
The first European Championship with any Chelsea involvement was in 1996, when football 'came home' to England. Our representation was limited to a pair of Scotland players, Craig Burley and John Spencer, plus Romania's Dan Petrescu and Russia keeper Dmitri Kharine – and all four of them exited at the group stage!

2000
Belgium and the Netherlands were on hosting duty for the first tournament of the new Millennium, and there were plenty more Chelsea players involved this time. Three of them went on to get their hands on the trophy, as Marcel Desailly, Didier Deschamps and Frank Leboeuf were in the France squad that beat Italy in the final.

2004
This time 10 Chelsea players were in action in Portugal and, remarkably, all but one of them made it out of the group stage. The last man standing was Bolo Zenden, who played not a minute of either of the Netherlands' knockout matches as they were eliminated at the semi-final stage, although Frank Lampard was a star for England with four goals.

2008
England were surprisingly absent from the tournament in Austria and Switzerland, but there were still plenty of Blues in action. Our involvement went all the way to the final thanks to Michael Ballack. Alas, the German midfielder's impressive (or should that be unimpressive?) collection of runners-up medals was added to once again...

2012
Another Euros, another shared hosting role – this time it was the turn of Poland and Ukraine, just a few weeks after the Blues had been crowned champions of Europe for the first time. Surprisingly, only seven of our triumphant squad were present at the tournament, but Spain had Juan Mata and Fernando Torres, and both scored in their dismantling of Italy in the final, with Torres' goal clinching him the Golden Boot.

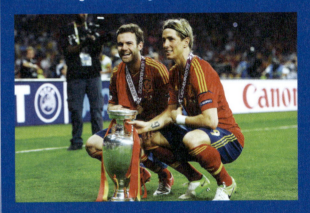

2016
The tally of Blues was down even further at France 2016, as only six made it. This time, there was to be no winner from the Chelsea ranks – indeed, nobody made it beyond the quarter-finals of this new 24-team format...

2020
The delayed Euro 2020, which was played all over the continent, finally took place in the summer of 2021 due to the Covid-19 pandemic. Chelsea were well represented once more, including in the final, as we had Mason Mount, Ben Chilwell and Reece James in the England squad hoping to 'bring football home'. But it was penalty heartache for the Three Lions, as an Italy side containing Jorginho and Emerson joined the list of Blues Euro winners over the years.

For

OFFICIAL
CLUB MERCHANDISE

visit the stadium megastore
or shop online at
chelseamegastore.com

RAHEEM STERLING

WORDSEARCH

Can you find all 12 names of these Chelsea players in the grid?

T	H	G	I	R	B	K	N	M	T	L	C
B	R	O	R	C	F	G	O	Z	W	L	G
Z	U	E	D	M	F	I	S	U	C	E	K
E	K	C	B	F	F	M	K	I	Q	W	T
D	N	T	H	H	E	H	C	D	M	L	I
Q	L	E	K	A	T	E	A	I	L	I	C
A	P	X	T	R	N	U	J	S	E	H	E
S	Y	O	O	I	R	A	C	A	M	C	S
B	N	T	V	I	E	W	N	S	J	E	N
W	K	E	U	T	I	R	H	I	M	V	O
M	A	D	U	E	K	E	T	A	B	B	B
N	K	U	N	K	U	G	J	A	E	S	M

BRIGHT   **NKUNKU**   **REITEN**

CUTHBERT   **BUCHANAN**   **CHILWELL**

JACKSON   **DISASI**   **JAMES**

KERR   **MACARIO**   **MADUEKE**

Answers on page 63

GURO REITEN

THE ULTIMATE STAMFORD BRIDGE QUIZ!

How much do you know about Chelsea's home? There's a point for each question below and a bonus point on offer to true Blues for the final question!

1 Can you name the famous end of Stamford Bridge that stands opposite the Matthew Harding End?

A: The Shed B: The Loft C: The Attic

2 George 'Gatling Gun' Hilsdon was the first player to score 100 goals for Chelsea, but what did they create at the stadium to celebrate his achievement?

A: Statue B: Weather vane C: Entrance sign

3 Chelsea's biggest home win of the Premier League era is 8-0, which we've recorded twice: once against Aston Villa and once against which team to secure the title in May 2010, when Didier Drogba (pictured) scored a hat-trick?

A: West Bromwich Albion
B: Wigan Athletic
C: Wolverhampton Wanderers

4 Who scored the goal that clinched the Premier League title for Chelsea in a 1-0 win over Crystal Palace at Stamford Bridge in May 2015?

A: John Terry
B: Didier Drogba
C: Eden Hazard

5 The biggest crowd for a competitive game at Stamford Bridge is 82,905, for a London derby back in 1935. Who were Chelsea playing that day?

A: Tottenham Hotspur
B: Arsenal
C: Fulham

6 What is the newest stand at Stamford Bridge?

A: West Stand B: East Stand
C: Matthew Harding Stand

7 Chelsea have played at Stamford Bridge throughout our history, but in what year was the club founded?

A: 1900 B: 1905 C: 1910

8 What is the name of the road in which Stamford Bridge is located?

A: Kings Road
B: Stamford Street
C: Fulham Road

9 There is a statue to one of our most popular players ever outside the entrance to the West Stand, but who is it?

A: Peter Osgood
B: Gianfranco Zola
C: Roy Bentley

10 Who is this player pictured celebrating our first home goal of the 2023/24 season?

A: Nicolas Jackson
B: Carney Chukwuemeka
C: Axel Disasi

BONUS POINT!

11 Score two points if you can correctly name our two mascots (pictured). There's no multiple choice to help you this time. Can you prove yourself to be a true Blue?

FINAL SCORE

Check the answers on page 63.

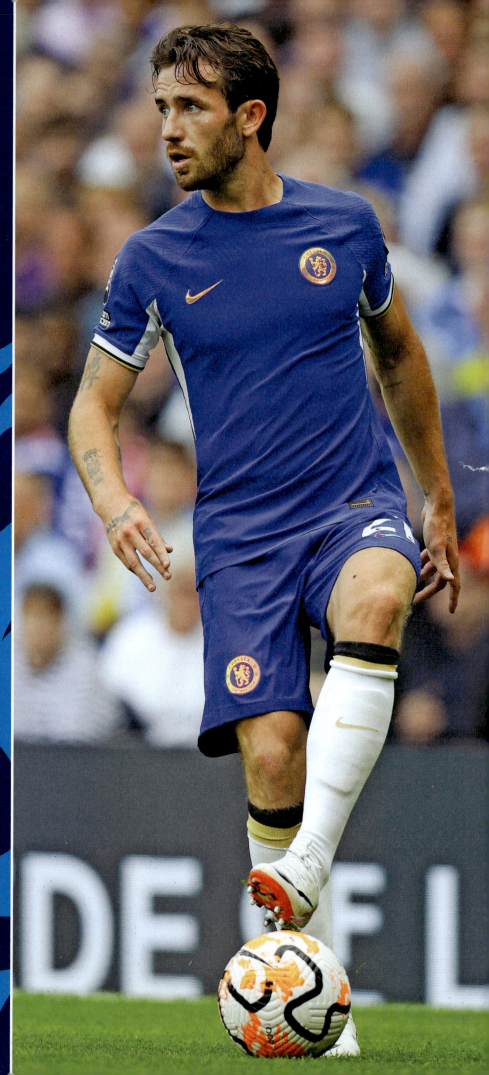

BEN CHILWELL